YOUR KNOWLEDGE HAS VALUE

- We will publish your bachelor's and master's thesis, essays and papers

- Your own eBook and book -
  sold worldwide in all relevant shops

- Earn money with each sale

Upload your text at www.GRIN.com
and publish for free

Bibliographic information published by the German National Library:

The German National Library lists this publication in the National Bibliography; detailed bibliographic data are available on the Internet at http://dnb.dnb.de .

This book is copyright material and must not be copied, reproduced, transferred, distributed, leased, licensed or publicly performed or used in any way except as specifically permitted in writing by the publishers, as allowed under the terms and conditions under which it was purchased or as strictly permitted by applicable copyright law. Any unauthorized distribution or use of this text may be a direct infringement of the author s and publisher s rights and those responsible may be liable in law accordingly.

Imprint:

Copyright © 2014 GRIN Verlag
Print and binding: Books on Demand GmbH, Norderstedt Germany
ISBN: 9783668743250

This book at GRIN:

https://www.grin.com/document/432045

Christian Horch

Institutional Change in Varieties of Capitalism. Temporary Employment in Germany

GRIN Verlag

GRIN - Your knowledge has value

Since its foundation in 1998, GRIN has specialized in publishing academic texts by students, college teachers and other academics as e-book and printed book. The website www.grin.com is an ideal platform for presenting term papers, final papers, scientific essays, dissertations and specialist books.

Visit us on the internet:

http://www.grin.com/

http://www.facebook.com/grincom

http://www.twitter.com/grin_com

Institutional Change in Varieties of Capitalism

Temporary Employment in Germany

Table of Contents

1. Introduction 2
2. Institutional Terrain and Institutional Stability 3
3. Institutional Change 4
4. Three Routes to Institutional Change 5
5. Temporary Employment in Germany 6
6. Conclusion 8
7. Bibliography 9

1. Introduction

In the face of globalization many states have been forced to adapt to the new challenges facing them in an ever more open market. The fact that markets increasingly escape the bounds of national economies and interact in international perspectives is apparent for example in the fields of "research, development and manufacturing activities" (Berger 2000, p. 44). These developments towards internationalization of economic and social policies and institutions lead in many cases to policies that adapt regulation to new international challenges or in other cases deregulate markets in a process of liberalization especially in the fields of labor and financial markets as well as training of workers, wage bargaining and education. Exemplary for the process of liberalization in the political economies over the last decades are the economic policies spearheaded by Margaret Thatcher in the United Kingdom and Ronald Reagan in the United States that transformed their respective economies radically towards more liberal practices. Especially the shift from industrialized economies towards ones that are more reliant on the service sector these adaptions are often unavoidable. (Berger 2000, pp. 43–46; Hall, Soskice 2001, pp. 2–6; Hall, Thelen 2009, p. 22).

Analyzing these processes and the impact of such policy changes on the political economies, societies and institutional frameworks has been the focus of research in both economics and political science – namely the Institutionalist branches. As such theoretical frameworks have been proposed in the literature of new institutional economy to explain the character of these changes and embed them in the interaction between the relevant actors – like institutions, government, firms and organizations. Therefore analyzing and explaining the differences and similarities between different national economies and their economic performance is at the center of the analysis. Here the Varieties of Capitalism approach proposed by Hall and Soskice provides a framework for understanding said differences and similarities of the political economies in the developed world. Opposed to the simple process of liberalization the VoC framework assumes the development of political economies towards the two arrangements of liberal market economies (LME) that feature a constellation characterized by competitive arrangements for coordination among actors whereas the model of coordinated market economies (CME) depend on collaborative arrangements (Hall, Soskice 2001, p. 8). Through this approach VoC provide insights on topics from "issues in innovation, vocational training, and corporate strategy to [...] legal systems, the development of social policy, and the stance nations take in international negotiations " (Hall and Soskice 2001, p. 2) while taking an actor-centered and rationalist approach.

The applicability of the VoC framework to explain institutional change has since come under criticism for oversimplifying the institutional reality and falling short of capturing the complexities of real-world changes in national political economies with their dichotomous separation into LMEs and CMEs (Campbell 2010, pp. 14ff). Hall and Thelen (2009) have however proposed an extension to the VoC framework to analyze institutional change in a more meaningful way by outlining modes of change along the assumption of institutional stability in accordance with the VoC framework. After outlining their approach this work aims to test the assumptions about institutional change in varieties of capitalism against the introduction of temporary work legislation in Germany to answer the question if a varieties of capitalism approach is able to explain this example of institutional change sufficiently. All of this while keeping in mind the CME present in Germany.

2. Institutional Terrain and Institutional Stability

The approach brought forward by Hall and Thelen (2009) aims to extend the VoC perspective with regards to institutional change and elaborate on both the nature and stability of institutions. To comprehend this perspective on institutional change it is at first necessary to outline the assumptions and understanding of institutions and the terrain in which they interact. In accordance with a wide range of literature on institutions (see North 1990; Hodgson 2006) there is are two ways in which institutions can function. Described "as a set of regularized practices with rule-like quality" (Hall, Thelen 2009, p. 9) they can be separated into formal and informal categories where the former describes for example the rule of law and other firmly graspable constraints and the latter refers to boundaries based on conventions and expectations.

Concerning the institutional terrain the two assumption are that on the one hand institutions serve not only as constraints, but also as bodies that provide actors with a range of possibilities to solve problems of collective action and provide opportunities. On the other hand they do not only provide the framework in which strategic action takes place and actors allocate resources, but also provide an entity for actors to interact with and use as a resource themselves. Importantly actors within a political economy are assumed to interact with institutions not for the common well-being, but to further their own interest – much as in a game-theoretic sense where cooperation or coordination is achieved not as a result of common understanding, but as the outcome that represents the intersection of the most favorable solution for each individual actor.

Considering this institutional terrain, the stability of institutions accordingly depends on institutions providing possibilities for actors to realize their self-interest. In context of the vast complexity of the institutional interdependencies the uncertainty of the implications of establishing new institutions is one factor of institutional stability. Actors will however test the boundaries of institutions and assess the risks and costs of defection from sanctioned behavior. This view stands in contrast to the functionalist assumption that stability is solely dependent on the institution's contribution to national welfare putting emphasis on actors pursuing self-interests and optimal outcomes (Hall, Thelen 2009, pp. 9–11).

Furthermore stability rests on the fact that adaption to institutions facilitates reliance on them. As actors organize their processes around existing institutions creating dependencies and interests connected with said institutions that were not present or intended when the institution was created (Campbell 2010, pp. 14–15; Hall, Thelen 2009, pp. 10–11).

3. Institutional Change

Deducted from these assumptions about institutional stability two key hypotheses about the agents and the impetus for institutional change can be deducted. First, there are multiple agents of adjustment that influence the construction, importance and development of institutions. On the one hand governments certainly have greater competences concerning the formal aspects of institutions as they can shape the institutional landscape thoroughly through regulations. Firms on the other hand through their behavior and strategies can shift importance from one institution to another and will do so more readily as economic survival may depend on it. Where firms have to adapt to international developments more rapidly governments will have to react. So as both actors are facing different pressures and inhibit different preferences they shape institutional change in the political economy.

4. Three Routes to Institutional Change

There are three routes Hall and Thelen outline that facilitate "institutional change in the political economy" (Hall, Thelen 2009, p. 15). These processes are namely reforms, defection and reinterpretation which each feature a distinctive dynamic (Hall, Thelen 2009, p. 1; p. 20f).

The dynamic of reform represents the process leading to institutional change that is specifically under the authority of governments. As a process that relies on coalitional politics the objective is to make out the actors involved in reaching support for institutional reform. Such actors working towards compromises can include different parties as for example political parties or firms represented by producer groups. Their interaction in a coalitional setting is characterized by distributive conflicts to which reforms of institutional change constantly have to be adjusted among the coalition's actors. These conflicts are furthermore always in context of existing institutions and the stance on reforms in one area of the institutional structure can always have an effect on an actor's position in a different area (Hall, Thelen 2009, pp. 20f).

Second, in the process of defection entails an actor, who was previously adhering to them, choosing to stop acting in accordance to the boundaries and practices set out by an institution. Furthermore a firm could choose to terminate membership in an association to open the possibility of restructuring internal processes to improve competitiveness that were previously impossible under the rules and boundaries set by the association. This process is in part comparable to the game-theoretic defection from a cooperation strategy (Hall, Thelen 2009, p. 18f).

Lastly, the dynamic of reinterpretation describes a change that does not inherently change the structure of the institutional environment – as reforms would in a top-down fashion – but that through a gradual process of transformation changes the purpose and interpretation of an institution's practices. In a step-by-step process formal law or regulation might be reinterpreted through the judiciary to shape institutional characteristics towards their set of interests (Hall, Thelen 2009, p. 19).

5. Temporary Employment in Germany

Defined by the OECD as "dependent employment of limited duration" (OECD Employment Outlook 2002, p. 170) temporary employment has been on the rise due to the constantly increasing competitiveness and instability in the global developed economies, thus creating the need to increase flexibility in working conditions as an instrument to adapt to these developments (Martínez et al. 2010, pp. 62–63). Although now common place temporary employment had been outlawed in post-war Germany until 1967. Up to 1967 mediating employees had been declared a matter of state authority.

But this date provides a first stage at which the institutional constraints concerning temporary employment were starting to change and could be analyzed as a process of reinterpretation. After opening their first subsidiary in Hamburg, Germany the Swiss temporary employment agency ADIA provided its services of mediating temporarily employed workers to other firms, but shortly after was forced to cease operations as German courts decided that their services were illegal under employment and social legislation. This decision was successfully appealed by ADIA in front of the Federal Constitutional Court (BVerfG) in 1967 leading to decision reducing government authority over employee mediation. This lead to a rapid increase in numbers of temporary employment agencies in the following years (Vitols 2003, p. 5f). This can be seen as an example supporting the assumption of institutional change from institutional stability accomplished through reinterpretation of existing legislation through courts, initiated by an entity interacting with said institution.

After the number of temporary employment agencies had increased it became apparent that regulation was not sufficient as criminal practices began to spread (Vitols 2003, p. 6).

Institutional change through reform was then introduced by the German Bundestag to accommodate the changing developments of the labor market and regulate the emerging sector with the "Arbeitnehmerüberlassungsgesetz" (Temporary Employment Act (TEA)) in 1972. This represented exhaustive regulation of the temporary employment market in regards to requiring state concessions and limiting the time frames for leases and re-leases for temporary employees (Vitols 2003, p. 7). Although early support for reform was mainly drawn from the political parties – the governing coalition of SPD and FPD (Social Democratic Party of Germany and Liberal Democratic Party) as well as the opposition consisting of the CDU/CSU (Christian Democratic/Social Union) were in favor of regulation – unions and other social actors were also mostly in favor of legislation, although they were not as consistently organized from the beginning. On the opposing side employer organizations were highly in favor of liberalizing regulation.

After 1972 the development of reforms is largely characterized by liberalization of the original TEA. The process of reforming the TAE from 1982 onwards is largely a representation of the political coalitions present in the German Bundestag during that time. Under conservative governments lead by the CDU/CSU who were in favor of temporary employment regulation many efforts in the form of reforms were taken to liberalize regulation towards more leniency for temporary employment agencies increasing their freedom to act (Vitols 2003, pp. 14–15). So during this period the coalition of the governing parties and employer associations presented a set of actors with common sets of interest that were able to produce institutional change through reforms.

Unions on the other hand were in a different position as they were in a position of conflicting interests. On the one hand their goal was to ensure adequate payment for temporarily employed workers, but on the other hand they also perceived them as a threat of replacing permanent staff represented by them (Vitols 2003, p. 31). This changed only after 2000.

After the legislation concerning temporary employment had mainly been liberalized after 1982 the coalition of the SPD and the Green Party managed to extend the discourse to include social actors from both unions and employer associations through the "Alliance for

Employment" in 2000 and to enact a reform through the "First Law for Modern Services in the Job Market" (Erstes Gesetz für modern Dienstleistungen am Arbeitsmarkt) in 2003 which strengthened the rights of temporarily employed workers making them more equal to permanent staff in social protection and wages. Unions were subsequently willing to negotiate with employer associations and for the first time included temporal employment workers in labor agreements (Vitols 2003, p. 31; Hamann 2011, pp. 30–31). While not specifically relevant to the framework presented this example stresses the importance of political coalitions across different spheres involved in the process of institutional change.

6. Conclusion

As was exemplified with the development of temporary employment in the German political economy Hall and Thelen provide a useful framework to understand institutional change. Especially the importance of political coalitions and firms as the initiators of change is observable in the way the legislature and regulations around temporary employment were revised and adapted. This extension to the VoC framework provides a perspective on the highly political process that shaped the evolution of the temporary employment legislature and how actors in different spheres influenced this change through processes that shifted "institutional practices 'from below'". The incremental changes observable in the regulations after 1972 in the case presented for German employment eventually lead to a major transformation of how employers are mediated and the way the associated institutions' boundaries and rules are changed. Although the extent of this work is in no way able to sufficiently subsume the development of temporary employment under the framework of institutional change in varieties of capitalism it might confirm the assumptions that institutional change in the current political economies of developed countries is not inherently one of liberalization and with the tools provided by Hall and Thelen can be analyzed in a more meaningful way.

7. Bibliography

OECD Employment Outlook 2002 (2002): OECD Publishing.

Berger, Suzanne (2000): G LOBALIZATION AND P OLITICS. In *Annu. Rev. Polit. Sci.* 3 (1), pp. 43–62. DOI: 10.1146/annurev.polisci.3.1.43.

Campbell, John L. (2010): Institutional reproduction and change. In *Oxford Handbook of Comparative Institutional Analysis*, pp. 87–115.

Hall, Peter A.; Soskice, David W. (2001): Varieties of capitalism. The institutional foundations of comparative advantage. Oxford [England], New York: Oxford University Press.

Hall, Peter A.; Thelen, Kathleen (2009): Institutional change in varieties of capitalism. In *Socio-Economic Review* 7 (1), pp. 7–34. DOI: 10.1093/ser/mwn020.

Hamann, Wolfgang (2011): Fremdpersonal im Unternehmen. 4., überarb. Aufl. Stuttgart [u.a.]: Boorberg (Schriftenreihe "Das Recht der Wirtschaft", 225).

Hodgson, Geoffrey (2006): What are Institutions? In *Journal of Economic Issues* 40(1), pp. 1–25.

Martínez, Gabriel; Cuyper, Nele de; Witte, Hans de (2010): Review of Temporary Employment Literature: Perspectives for Research and Development in Latin America Revisión de la Literatura sobre Trabajo Temporal: Perspectivas para la Investigación y el Desarrollo en América Latina. In *Psykhe* 19 (1), pp. 61–73.

North, Douglass Cecil (1990): Institutions, institutional change and economic performance. Cambridge [etc.]: Cambridge university press (Political economy of institutions and decisions).

Vitols, Katrin (2003): Die Regulierung der Zeitarbeit in Deutschland. Vom Sonderfall zur Normalbranche (No. 5). Available online at http://nbn-resolving.de/urn:nbn:de:0168-ssoar-111749.

YOUR KNOWLEDGE HAS VALUE

- We will publish your bachelor's and master's thesis, essays and papers

- Your own eBook and book - sold worldwide in all relevant shops

- Earn money with each sale

Upload your text at www.GRIN.com
and publish for free